POETICA 29

Goethe: Roman Elegies

Poetica is a series of texts, translations
and miscellaneous works relating to
poetry of all ages and cultures.

Other books by Michael Hamburger
published by Anvil Press Poetry

POETRY
Roots in the Air
Collected Poems 1941–1994

LITERARY CRITICISM
The Truth of Poetry

TRANSLATIONS
An Unofficial Rilke
Poems of Paul Celan
Hölderlin: Poems and Fragments

Johann Wolfgang von Goethe

ROMAN ELEGIES
and other poems

Selected, translated and with an introduction by
MICHAEL HAMBURGER

ANVIL PRESS POETRY

T 122157

Published in 1996
by Anvil Press Poetry Ltd
69 King George Street London SE10 8PX

Revised and expanded from *Poems and Epigrams* 1983

ISBN 085646 274 8

This book is published with financial assistance
from The Arts Council of England

A CIP record of this title is available from the British Library

Designed and composed in Ehrhardt
by Anvil Press Poetry Ltd
Printed and bound in England
by Morganprint (Blackheath) Ltd

ACKNOWLEDGEMENTS

We thank Suhrkamp / Insel Publishers Inc., Boston, USA, for permission to include eight of the *Roman Elegies* which were commissioned for Goethe, *Selected Poems* (edited by Christopher Middleton), published by Suhrkamp / Insel in their twelve-volume *Selected Writings of Goethe*, and Dr Siegfried Unseld of Suhrkamp Verlag, Frankfurt, for permission to include other translations originally published in that volume.

Contents

Later Poems

from *West–Eastern Divan* (1814–19)

Miscellaneous Epigrams

Introduction

THE EARLIEST VERSION of a Goethe poem I have found among my papers was done in 1939, at the age of fifteen. Intermittently I have been translating Goethe ever since, but it took the 150th anniversary of Goethe's death in 1832 to prod me into collecting these versions. The juvenile one is excluded, if only because I no longer like its original, 'Das Göttliche'; but I have now been able to add all the later translations excluded from the first edition of this book, because they were due to appear in an edition of Goethe's selected works in English then being prepared in America. If even the present gathering of all but my juvenile versions of poems by Goethe remains miscellaneous in character, one reason is that I have never been able to translate Goethe as persistently and consistently as I translated his younger contemporary Hölderlin; and all my repeated attempts suggest that much of Goethe's best poetry is hardly translatable into English. The evidence of two centuries of English Goethe renderings points to the same conclusion. Most of his lyrical poetry remains virtually unknown outside the schools and universities. *Faust* is translated again and again; but no single version has established itself as a standard text in the English-speaking world.

To reflect on the untranslatability and elusiveness of Goethe's poetic work as a whole is to go straight to the heart of his uniqueness, his staggering diversity and the extent to which many of his most original poems – especially the earlier lyrics – are inextricably rooted in their own linguistic humus. Though I hope that even the small selection that follows will at least intimate the range and scope of Goethe's shorter poems, the selection could not be a balanced one, because those songs and ballads in which Goethe came closest to folksong defied translation – and so did many of the poems of his middle and later years that go to the opposite extreme of intricately formal artifice.

The unity within the diversity of Goethe's work has been looked for mainly in his personality, which was documented with unprecedented diligence even in his lifetime – not without his connivance. Yet the 'open secret' of Goethe's unity seems to me to lie elsewhere: not in the ego so disliked by many of his readers and critics – the 'disagreeable, egotistical man and overrated writer' whom Patrick

White's Waldo, of *The Solid Mandala*, must have encountered in the *Conversations with Eckermann* or a biography rather than Goethe's own works – but in the degree to which Goethe's ego was always a vehicle for the 'it', whose discovery by Groddeck followed that psychologist's immersion in Goethe's works. 'There's something anonymous in it,' Goethe wrote in his old age about the identity we think we designate by people's names. The same is true of Goethe's poetry, even at its most confessional and seemingly most subjective. Folksong was only one of the many models to which Goethe resorted in the course of his long productive life as vehicles for the 'it', for the anonymous components in his own personality. What remained constant in his work, whatever the literary models or precedents, was his almost mystical faith in the hidden connections between one thing and another, between every thing and every other, in a cosmos that contains so much variety, conflict and transmutation within its unity. His scientific pursuits sprang from the same faith; and, conscious though he was of his excellence and achievements in so many different fields – including all the literary *genres* – in the end he saw himself only as the human being of his little epitaphs – a 'representative' and 'universal' man only because he had been a vehicle for so much that is universal in human and non-human nature.

Throughout his diverse modes and phases, too, Goethe remained a master of the vernacular. Other poets, the more translatable, cultivated one personal idiom that became so much their own as to be imitable even in another language: Hölderlin and Rilke are lyrical poets of that kind in German. Goethe cultivated every stratum of the spoken and written language, as well as creating neologisms and breaking the very conventions he had previously established, but returned in the casual verse of his old age to a diction so plain and demotic as to be impersonal. Poetic distinction mattered no more to him at this stage – in his late rhymed epigrams or 'sayings' – than personal distinction. He would have liked these rhymed epigrams to become proverbial – to be everyone's property. That few of them have become so in their own language, let alone in the 'world literature' that became so important to him in his last years, shows up the hollowness of nineteenth-century attempts to turn Goethe into a national institution and educational paragon, by monumentalizing him. A microcosm himself, Goethe knew that he was 'at the centre' of his cosmos even in the smallest, least macrocosmic of his writings; but nineteenth-century notions of 'grandeur' confused his classicism with his classicizing and found exemplariness mainly in his most overtly didactic passages. Yet as late as the early twentieth century, German schoolmasters were embarrassed even by *Faust*, and mint copies of the first edition of Goethe's *West-Eastern Divan* could be picked up in German bookshops up to the First World War, almost a century after its publication, while the monuments and secondary literature mounted up.

If my choice of poems seems eccentric to those versed in the more official canon, it will be because I was not guided by considerations of 'major' and 'minor' work. I translated those poems I was moved – and able – to translate in my own fashion, a strictly empathetic one, as wary of additions to the text as of subtractions from it. A great many total failures narrowed down my choice; and a few partial failures were admitted, where the right rhymes did not present themselves, and that subtraction left something substantial or essential enough to do justice to Goethe's wisdom, if not to his art. By no means all the roughage in my versions has been added by me; but several of his most delicate poems were among the total failures.

GOETHE'S OWN arrangement of his poems, towards the end of his life, was generic and thematic rather than strictly chronological, though to some extent the two orders overlap, because each phase of Goethe's development favoured certain poetic forms. Yet songs at one end of his gamut, epigrams at the other, were recurrent media throughout his working life. In the 1770s, when he broke the mould of conventional, Rococo social verse, with the help of a characteristically wide and heterogeneous range of models, his strength lay in improvised forms. During the so-called 'classical' phase of his middle years he tended more towards set forms, classical elegy and epigram, the sonnet and Italianate rhymed stanza. By his old age he had assimilated oriental modes, Chinese and Indian as well as the Persian and Arabian ones of the *West-Eastern Divan*, but returned to irregular rhymed improvisations in many of his songs, epigrams and occasional pieces. That development is bound up with Goethe's constant dialectic of Art and Nature, Reason and Energy, Order and Freedom. In his breakthrough of the 1770s Nature, Energy and Freedom erupted with such vehemence as to leave little room for their opposites. During the reaction that followed his *Sturm und Drang*, Goethe went so far as to reject the 'half-nonsense' of his 'Wayfarer's Storm Song' from a collection of his works. In old age he became reconciled to all his phases and their excesses – even to Werther, the suicidal hero of his most popular work before *Faust*, and one that had been an acute embarrassment to him in his middle years; for 'the road of excess' had indeed led Goethe to 'the palace of wisdom'. The 'Wayfarer's

Storm Song', too, was readmitted to the canon, as a work appropriate to one phase of the development which Goethe, the student of nature, affirmed as a primal necessity in every microcosm and macrocosm – from the universal to the national and individual.

The dithyrambic 'Wandrers Sturmlied' was written at the height of Goethe's *Sturm und Drang* glorification of Energy, titanic revolt and what would have been unbridled individualism, if from the first Goethe had not been a vehicle for the 'it' or 'id'. In the original text the force invoked in that poem is not 'genius' – which in German is denoted by the French loan-word *genie* – but the Latin *genius* or Greek *daimon*, a spirit. Yet for Goethe the two were one. His consciousness, at this early period, of his own genius was inseparable from his awareness of a force greater than himself, a cosmic force. To be open to that force, to allow it to operate within oneself, was 'genius'. A seeming mistranslation of Goethe's word 'Genius' in the poem was called for to render that seminal concurrence. 'Wayfarer's Storm Song' is Goethe's most whole-hearted, most thorough-going celebration of the 'it', of the life-force, in his early work. His love songs of the same period celebrate it too, but in a manner that does not break nearly as drastically with the conventions of polite prosody or good sense, since erotic verse had never ceased since antiquity to break through every kind of convention.

Poetically, the celebration was made possible by the fruitful misunderstanding of Pindar's prosody and diction in eighteenth-century Germany. Not only the free verse of Goethe's poem, but its rhapsodic, elliptic syntax – which anticipates some of the innovations of the German Expressionist writers of this century – derives from this misunderstanding. It gave Goethe and his *Sturm und Drang* contemporaries the very licence they needed for a liberation of their form and diction from all the restraints of rational discourse and literary decorum which Goethe himself had observed in his juvenile Rococo period. The language of this dithyramb, therefore, could enact another of Goethe's constant unifying tenets – the reciprocity of world and self, of inner and outer energies. That the inner energies are raw, unprocessed feelings here, rather than the differentiated ones derived from the minute study of natural and human phenomena, distinguishes this early phase from the later and last phases of Goethe's work. The nature, cosmic and human, of this poem is a sheer dynamism – opposed by a temporarily broken circuit in the protagonist. That break in the circuit may be due to ratiocination or individuation or an awareness of social inhibitions, unknown to the 'small dark fiery peasant' – Rousseau's natural man; but it will be repaired only by reciprocity, by the capacity of the human heart to generate a corresponding charge of heat, energy, courage.

The poem was bound to strike Goethe as barbarous when, together with Schiller, he had taken on the task of civilizing German taste and making up for the Augustan classicism missing from German literature for historical reasons. The turbulence of his early free-verse poems – he was to write others more consonant with the educational mission he had assumed at Weimar – was incompatible with a classicizing aesthetic derived mainly from Winckelmann and the related ethos of enlightened humanism. Another century had to pass before Nietzsche vindicated both Goethe's early dithyrambs and Hölderlin's insights into the character of the ancient Greeks; and, Greek scholar though he was, Nietzsche wrote dithyrambs more Goethean than Pindaric. As far as Goethe's development is concerned, no digging into the Dionysian layers in pre-Socratic Greece was required to reconcile him to the intuitions that had gone into the writing of such verse; they belonged to one stage in an evolution that had to encompass and balance extreme antinomies. In his old age he could return to his early subject Faust, casting classical light into its Gothic gloom, so that all the metamorphoses of a lifetime would be contained within a single work, and his beginning linked to his end.

IN FACE OF the untranslatability, for me, of most of Goethe's best-known lyrics and ballads of his early and middle years, all I could hope to achieve in this gathering of poems is to give its readers an intimation of Goethe's thematic range, from youth to old age. To so much as intimate Goethe's incomparable range of kinds, forms, tones and moods I should have had to include narrative poems on the one hand, dramatic fragments or monologues on the other; and some hundreds of lyrics, epigrams, reflective and occasional poems. The occasional character of so much of Goethe's poetry, as of the dramatic work he produced in his capacity of theatre director at Weimar, shows to what extent he remained a truly classical, as distinct from classicizing, writer in a Romantic age – a writer who could be true to himself while turning his hand to any sort of work that was needed. If my selection has a bias, it is towards that happy versatility rather than to the more familiar image of Goethe as producer of 'fragments of a great confession'. Yet the difference is one of emphasis only, with a writer who came to have little use for the banal dichotomy of subjective and objective concerns, whose scientific pursuits were inseparable from his poetic ones, and whose wisdom drew not only on vision and imagination but on decades of practical experience in the minutiae of administration.

Even before that experience became available to him, at the time of his *Sturm und Drang* breakthrough, Goethe's versatility was more remarkable than his cultivation of any particular *genre* or form. Love poems that owed their organic, expressive rhythms and unliterary diction to the liberating example of folksong alternated with *persona* poems, like the 'Prometheus' or 'Ganymede', deriving from a very personal response to Greek myths. Reflective and occasional poems, even squibs like 'Dinner at Koblenz' or 'Reviewer' in this selection, were also in evidence, as was the humour that Goethe never felt to be incongruous with the utmost seriousness – even with the mystical solemnity to which he could rise in *Faust* or some of the lyrics of the *West-Eastern Divan*. That is my excuse for mixing the kinds, manners and tones in this book, with a specimen or two of Goethe's humour at its earthiest and most demotic, from the late epigrams. Goethe was sure enough of his centre, his complicity with nature – in which nothing is great or small, crucial or marginal – to permit himself the same freedom and mobility in art. If this characteristic of Goethe's retains its power to shock us, so much the better: to be shocked is a state close to that wonderment which Goethe himself treasured and retained right into his old age.

For related reasons I have included those of the *Roman Elegies* – or *Erotica Romana*, as Goethe originally called them – which have remained absent from most editions of Goethe's works ever since they were written, only because they touch on the sexual act as such and on venereal disease. Goethe's freedom from inhibitions in sexual matters – homosexuality and impotence occur elsewhere in his poetry, and he took over a homoerotic convention from his Persian models for the *West-Eastern Divan*, as in the poem 'Summer Night' included here – is only one aspect, though a telling one, of his pervasive acceptance of the whole of human and non-human nature. By this I am far from meaning that there are no moral discriminations or gradations in his work; on the contrary, his work is full of them, because his world was one of concentric spheres, each of which must be governed by the laws appropriate to it. In love, as in all things, Goethe wanted progression – from the merely sensual to the intellectual and spiritual planes. For all his 'pagan' pantheism, too, Goethe did not glorify male eroticism at the expense of the female. From the early *persona* poem 'In Court' – thematically related to the Gretchen complex in *Faust* that culminates in the celebration of the 'eternally Feminine' – Goethe's work was revolutionary in its stress on the feminine principle, whether embodied in individual women quite as differentiated as his male characters or in the diverse goddesses of his pantheon, not excluding Nature,

Imagination and Wisdom. This dedication alone sets him apart from the primitivists of a would-be sexual liberation.

I CAN ONLY hope that there is no need to apologize again for defying English prejudice against adaptations of classical metres, such as the elegiac couplets of Goethe's *Roman Elegies* and *Venetian Epigrams*. That any modern adaptation of those metres turns them into something other than what they were in Greek and Latin poetry, goes without saying; but the same applies to English adaptations of any metre derived from French or Italian models, such as the sonnet. For myself I can say only that I welcome any alternative to the iambic beat that has been so nearly worked to death in the course of the centuries, though English iambics have permitted a degree of irregularity that Goethe and Schiller would have done well to imitate, especially in their dramatic blank verse; and that I have not found English elegiacs or hexameters more refractory than any of the other metres that Goethe used – and there is scarcely a metre he did not try out at one time or another, as well as extemporizing his own. Feminine rhymes tend to dominate in much of Goethe's rhymed verse. Not only is English much poorer in those rhymes than German, with its inflections, but in English they tend towards comic effects, of which Byron was a master. Such effects were admissible in some of the poems of the *West-Eastern Divan*, where a playful mobility – the virtuosity of old age – overrides all considerations of gravity or lightness; but the 'Apothegmata. Orphic', for instance, needed those feminine rhymes which I could not provide within my self-imposed limits of semantic faithfulness. Those poems are a summary of Goethe's thinking about law and liberty, necessity and choice. I could have made prettier versions of them by letting myself go, but at the expense of Goethe's own austerity in these poems. Elsewhere, as in a few lines of the *Roman Elegies* and all the epigrams, more semantic latitude was permissible. In the second 'Mignon Song' I changed Goethe's 'Sehnsucht' to 'loss', which is the precondition of the yearning or nostalgia of the German text, not the feeling itself, because a more precise rendering did not fit into the metre, and the feeling is adequately conveyed by the whole poem, without being named. To make up for that, I was able to transpose the very recurrent rhyme that threads Goethe's poem.

Nonetheless, I am not offering 'English poems in their own right' here, but pointers to the original texts, inductions to them for persons with little or no German. If one or two of my versions also stand up as poems in English, that is a bonus, a stroke of luck. English poetry is so rich as to have little need or room for additions in the guise of translations; but our awareness of 'world literature' is not rich enough to do without a poet as extraordinary and as central as Goethe, whose range of insight, knowledge and penetration exceeded that of any other poet of his age. If this book serves only to arouse curiosity about a writer so many-sided as to constitute a whole literature, it will have served its purpose. To satisfy that curiosity has proved a lifetime occupation for generations of readers and scholars; yet elusive as Goethe's totality is, with its irreducible component of anonymity, it can be grasped imaginatively in the tiniest of its parts.

MICHAEL HAMBURGER
Suffolk, March 1982; April 1996

MISCELLANEOUS POEMS

Wayfarer's Storm Song

Whom you do not abandon, Genius,
Neither rain nor storm
Will breathe terror upon his heart.
Whom you do not abandon, Genius,
The raincloud,
The hailblizzard
Will sing towards
As the lark
Up above.

Whom you do not abandon, Genius,
You will lift over the quagpath
With your wings of fire.
He will wander
As with flower feet
Over Deucalion's flood mire,
Killing Python, lithe, great,
Pythius Apollo.

Whom you do not abandon, Genius,
Woollen wings you will spread beneath
When on the rock he sleeps,
With guardian wings will cover him
In the grove's midnight.

Whom you do not abandon, Genius,
In the snow flurry
You will wrap in warmth.
For warmth the Muses make,
For warmth the Graces.

*

Hover around me, Muses,
And you, Graces!
This is water, this is earth
And the son of water and earth
Over whom I pass
Godlike.

You are pure as the heart of the waters,
You are pure as the marrow of earth,
You hover about me, and I hover
Across water and earth
Godlike.

Shall he return,
The small dark fiery peasant!
Shall he return, expecting
Only your gifts, Father Bromius,
And brightly shining radiant fire,
He return bravely,
And I, whom you escort,
All you Muses and Graces,
Whom all things await that you,
Muses and Graces,
Garlanding bliss
Have glorified throughout life,
Return disheartened?

Father Bromius,
You are Genius,
Century's Genius,
Are what inward ardour
Was to Pindar,
What to the world
Phoebus Apollo is.
Ah me! Ah me! Inward warmth,
Soul warmth,

Centre,
Glow towards
Phoebus Apollo,
Or coldly else
His princely glance
Will glide over and past you.
Struck by envy
Will linger on the cedar's might
That does not wait
For him to put out verdure.

Why last does my song name you,
You out of whom it began?
You in whom it will end,
You from whom it springs,
Jupiter Pluvius!
You, you my song pours out
And Castalian Spring
Flows, a tributary stream,
Flows for idle
Mortally happy ones
Away from you,
Who seizing cover me,
Jupiter Pluvius.

Not by the elm tree
You visited him –
With the pair of doves
In your tender arms,
Garlanded with the affable rose,
Him, that playful flowerglad
Anacreon,
Storm-breathing deity.
Not in the poplar wood
On Sybaris' shore
On the mountain range's

Sun-drenched brow did
You seize him,
That bee-humming,
Honey-babbling
Kindly beckoning
Theocritus.

When the wheels rushed
Wheel to wheel, swiftly on to the goal
High flew
Victory-transfused
The whips' crack of youths,
And dust whirled
As down from a mountain range
Scree does into the valley,
Your soul glowed dangers, Pindar,
Courage. – Glowed. –
Poor heart –
There on the hill,
Celestial energy,
Only ardour enough –
My cottage yonder –
To wade there.

Prometheus

Cover your heaven, Zeus,
With cloudy vapours
And like a boy
Beheading thistles
Practise on oaks and mountain peaks –
Still you must leave
My earth intact
And my small hovel, which you did not build,
And this my hearth
Whose glowing heat
You envy me.

I know of nothing more wretched
Under the sun than you gods!
Meagrely you nourish
Your majesty
On dues of sacrifice
And breath of prayer
And would suffer want
But for children and beggars,
Poor hopeful fools.

Once too, a child,
Not knowing where to turn,
I raised bewildered eyes
Up to the sun, as if above there were
An ear to hear my complaint,
A heart like mine
To take pity on the oppressed.

*

Who helped me
Against the Titans' arrogance?
Who rescued me from death,
From slavery?
Did not my holy and glowing heart,
Unaided, accomplish all?
And did it not, young and good,
Cheated, glow thankfulness
For its safety to him, to the sleeper above?

I pay homage to you? For what?
Have you ever relieved
The burdened man's anguish!
Have you ever assuaged
The frightened man's tears?
Was it not omnipotent Time
That forged me into manhood,
And eternal Fate,
My masters and yours?

Or did you think perhaps
That I should hate this life,
Flee into deserts
Because not all
The blossoms of dream grew ripe?

Here I sit, forming men
In my image,
A race to resemble me:
To suffer, to weep,
To enjoy, to be glad –
And never to heed you,
Like me!

Dinner at Koblenz

Between Lavater and Basedow
I sat at table, my spirits not low.
Our Mr Deacon, loath to lag,
Quickly mounted a jet-black nag,
Sat a vicar behind him on the horse
And for that Revelation took his course
Which John the Prophet took good care
To seal for us with enigmas most rare;
He broke those seals with no more ado
Than a treacle tin would demand from you,
And let his holy cane unfurl
The four-square city and the gates of pearl
For his disciple, all in a whirl.
Meanwhile, no traveller, I had put away
A piece of salmon, quietly.

Father Basedow, in the interim,
Puts a dancing master next to him
And shows him clearly, clause by clause,
What to Christ and the Apostles baptism was;
And why it is not seemly now
To sprinkle water on an infant's brow.
This made the other angry and sore,
He wouldn't listen to any more
And said that every child could see
The Bible proved the contrary.
I blithely meanwhile had polished off
A whole roast cockerel, tender enough.

And, as to Emmaus, on they fare,
At fire and spirit speed unriddle,
Prophets beside me, here and there,
This world's own child in the middle.

Reviewer

There was a fellow dropped in for lunch,
Didn't bother me much, I just let him munch,
Had the kind of meal I have every day;
The fellow gorged himself mightily
And for dessert ate up what I'd stored.
But as soon as he'd left my larder cleared,
The devil led him to my neighbour's, where
After this fashion he discussed the fare:
'The soup might have been more piquantly spiced,
The roast more crisp, the wine better iced.'
A curse on that damnable knave, that evil-doer!
Put the dog to sleep. He's a book reviewer.

In Court

Who gave it to me, I will not tell,
The child inside my womb. –
Shameful! You spit: that harlot there! –
But I'm honest all the same.

To whom I was pledged, I will not tell.
My sweetheart's a dear good chap.
Whether he wears a gold chain round his neck
Or wears a labourer's cap.

If scorn and mockery have to be borne,
I'll bear them all alone.
I know him well, he knows me well,
And God knows all we've done.

Mr Parson, Mr Magistrate,
Leave off, please, let me be.
My child it is, my child it remains,
And you'll not help it or me.

Gipsy Song

from the early draft of the play *Götz von Berlichingen*

In the foggy drizzle, in the deep snow,
In the wild wood, in the winter night
I heard the howling of hungry wolves,
I heard the brown owl cry.
    Willy wow wow wow!
    Willy wo wo wo!
    Wito who!

One day I shot a cat on the fence,
It was Anne the witch's darling black cat;
So at night seven werewolves came to me,
There were seven seven hags in the village.
    Willy wow wow wow!
    Willy wo wo wo!
    Wito who!

I knew them all, I knew them well.
There was Kate and Betty and old Anne,
There was Madge and Barbara, Eve and Jane;
They crouched in a circle and howled at me.
    Willy wow wow wow!
    Willy wo wo wo!
    Wito who!

Then I called each one out loud by her name:
What is it, Anne? what is it, Jane?
So they shook themselves and betook themselves
Back home, and howled as they ran:
    Willy wow wow wow!
    Willy wo wo wo!
    Wito who!

'All things the gods bestow'

All things the gods bestow, the infinite ones,
On their darlings completely,
All the joys, the infinite ones,
All the pains, the infinite ones, completely.

Wayfarer's Night Song

Over the hilltops all
Is still,
Hardly a breath
Seems to ruffle
Any tree crest;
In the wood not one small bird's song.
Only wait, before long
You too will rest.

My Goddess

Which of the immortals
Merits the greatest praise?
I'll dispute with no one,
But I award it
To the ever-active,
Ever-new,
Bizarrest daughter of Jove,
His darling child,
Imagination.

For her he's endowed
With every caprice
That else he reserves
For himself alone,
And takes pleasure in
The girl's foolish ways.

Rose-garlanded
With her lily-stalk
She may walk
Wildflower valleys,
Command the summer birds
And with bee lips
From blossom sip
Lightly nourishing dew,
Or with hair flying
And glowering eyes
May ride in the wind,
Rush around rock face
And thousand-hued
Like morning and evening,
Always changing

Like moon glances
Appear to mortals.

Let us all
Praise the Father,
The ancient, exalted,
Who deigned to join
Mere mortal men
To so beautiful,
Unaging a consort.

For us alone
To her he has bound
With celestial bonds
And enjoined her
As a faithful spouse
Never to leave
The happy or wretched man.

All the other
Piteous kinds
Of our prolific
Living earth
Roam and forage
In dark enjoyment
Or murky pain
Of their momentary
Restricted lives,
Bowed under the yoke
Of immediate need.

But to us he's entrusted
His most resourceful,
His dandled daughter.

*

Be grateful for that!
Tenderly look on her
As you look on a mistress!
Grant her the dignity
Of a household's lady!

And, whatever you do,
Keep your mother-in-law,
Old Prudence, from ever
Slighting the delicate soul!

Yet I know her sister,
The elder, less flighty one,
My quiet friend –
O may she only turn
Away from me when
The light of this life does,
She who nobly impels
And comforts us: Hope!

Anacreon's Grave

Where the rose is in flower, where vines interlace with the laurel,
    Where the turtle-dove calls, where the small cricket delights,
What a grave is this, which all the gods have embellished,
    Graced and planted with life? It is Anacreon's rest.
Springtime, summer, and autumn blessed the fortunate poet:
    And from winter the mound kept him secure in the end.

Night Thoughts

You I pity, twice unhappy stars,
Being lovely, blessed with bright effulgence,
Gladly shedding light for ships in danger,
Yet by gods and mortals unrewarded:
Love you cannot, never yet knew love!
But incessantly eternal hours
Move your ranks through vast celestial spaces.
Oh, what distant journeys you've completed
Since, reposing in my loved one's arms,
You and midnight wholly I forgot.

Human Limits

When the most ancient
Heavenly Father
From rolling clouds
With a calm hand scatters
Lightning flashes like seed
Over the earth,
I kiss the lowest
Hem of his garment,
A childlike awe
Steadfast within me.

For against gods
No man alive
Should measure himself.
If he rises up
And with the crown of his head
Touches the stars,
Nowhere then do the groping
Soles of his feet adhere,
But clouds and winds
Make him their game.

If with firm,
Marrowy bones he stands
On the well-founded
Durable earth,
Not with so much as the oak
Or the vine
He can presume
To compare his height.

What distinguishes
Gods from human kind?
That many waves
Move on before gods,
An eternal tide;
Us the wave lifts,
Us the wave engulfs,
And we go down.

A little ring
Confines our lives,
And many generations
For ever they link
On to their being's
Infinite chain.

The Mignon Songs

from the novel *Wilhelm Meisters Lehrjahre*, 1783-1796

I

Do you know the land where the lemon trees flower,
Golden oranges glow in the dark-leaved bower,
Where a gentle wind blows from an azure sky,
Unruffled the myrtle grows and the laurels rise high –
Do you know the land?
　　　　There, only there
With you, my belovèd, I long to go.

Do you know the house? Pillared, its roof reclines,
The great hall gleams and brightly the white room shines,
And marble statues look down, their gaze is mild:
'What have they done to you, tell me, my poor child!' –
Do you know the house?
　　　　There, only there
With you, my protector, I long to go.

Do you know the mountain and its cloudy track?
Slowly in the mist the mule gropes its way back,
In caves the ancient brood of the dragons teems,
Rocks come tumbling down, above them roaring streams –
Do you know the rocks?
　　　　There, only there
Our way can lead; O Father, let us go!

II

None but whom loss has rent
Knows what I suffer.
In lonely banishment,
Dead to all pleasure,
I search the sky, intent

On one direction.
Oh! but far off he went
Who loves and knows me.
I reel; hot pangs torment
My heart and entrails.
None but whom loss has rent
Knows what I suffer.

III

Then, seeming, let me come to be,
Do not take off me the white gown!
From lovely earth now willingly
To a firm house I hurry down.

There a small stillness long I'll bide,
Until I open eyes all new
And leave the wrappings, purified,
The girdle and the wreath, for you.

To those above, the heavenly shapes,
Woman or man, it's all the same,
No dress or pleated covering drapes
A body's bare, transfigured frame.

*

Exempt from drudgery, common fears,
Deep pain enough in life I bore;
Grief made me older than my years –
Now make me young for ever more.

The Harpist Songs

from the novel *Wilhelm Meisters Lehrjahre*, 1783-1796

I

Who never mixed with tears his bread,
Who never through the dead night hours
Sat weeping on his lonely bed,
He does not know you, heavenly powers.

You lead us on; by you incited,
A wretched mortal will transgress.
And then you leave him comfortless;
For every earthly wrong's requited.

II

The man whom loneliness once receives,
Soon that man is alone;
Everyone loves, everyone lives
And leaves the man to moan.

Yes, leave me to my pain.
If once I can remain
Utterly on my own,
I shall not be alone.

A lover listens, slinking like a thief,
Whether his girl friend's alone.
So into me, by night and by day,
The lonely, slinks grief,

The lonely, slinks pain.
Oh, never, never again,
Till buried I lie on my own
Will it leave me alone!

III

To the doorways I will slink,
Humbly stand there, quietly;
Good folk hand me food and drink,
Then I shall be on my way.

All of them when I appear
Will feel happier than they did.
They will weep a single tear,
And I wonder why it's shed.

Nearness of the Belovèd

I think of you when from the sea the shimmer
 Of sunlight streams;
I think of you when on the brook the dimmer
 Moon casts her beams.

I see your face when on the distant highway
 Dust whirls and flakes,
In deepest night when on the mountain byway
 The traveller quakes.

I hear your voice when, dully roaring, yonder
 Waves rise and spill;
Listening, in silent woods I often wander
 When all is still.

I walk with you, though miles from you divide me;
 Yet you are near!
The sun goes down, soon stars will shine to guide me.
 Would you were here!

ROMAN ELEGIES

I

Deign to speak to me, stones, you high palaces, deign to address me,
    Streets, now say but one word! Genius, will you not stir?
True, all is living yet within your sanctified precincts,
    Timeless Rome; only me all still in silence receives.
Oh, who will whisper to me, at what small window, revealing
    Her, the dear one, whose glance, searing, will quicken my blood?
Can I not guess on what roads, forever coming and going,
    Only for her sake I'll spend all my invaluable time?
Still I'm seeing the sights, the churches, the ruins, the columns,
    As a serious man ought to and does use his days.
That, however, will pass; and soon no more than one temple,
    Amor's temple alone, claim this initiate's zeal.
Rome, you remain a whole world; but a world without love would not ever
    Truly amount to the world, neither would Rome still be Rome.

Ia

Fortune beyond my loveliest daydreams fulfilled is my own now,
    Amor, my clever guide, passed all the palaces by.
Long he has known, and I too had occasion to learn by experience,
    What a richly gilt room hides behind hangings and screens.
You may call him a boy and blind and ill-mannered, but, clever
    Amor, I know you well, never corruptible god!
Us they did not take in, those façades so imposing and pompous,
    Gallant balcony here, dignified courtyard down there.
Quickly we passed them by, and a humble but delicate doorway
    Opened to guided and guide, made them both welcome within.
All he provides for me there, with his help I obtain all I ask for,
    Fresher roses each day strewn on my path by the god.
Isn't it heaven itself? – And what more could the lovely Borghese,
    Nipotima herself offer a lover than that?
Dinners, drives and dances, operas, card games and parties,
    Often merely they steal Amor's most opportune hours.
Airs and finery bore me; when all's said and done, it's the same thing
    Whether the skirt you lift is of brocade or of wool.
Or if the wish of a girl is to pillow her lover in comfort,
    Wouldn't he first have her put all those sharp trinkets away?
All those jewels and pads, and the lace that surrounds her, the whalebone,
    Don't they all have to go, if he's to feel his belovèd?
Us it gives much less trouble! Your plain woollen dress in a jiffy,
    Unfastened by me, slips down, lies in its folds on the floor.
Quickly I carry the child in her flimsy wrapping of linen,
    As befits a good nurse, teasingly, into her bed.
Bare of silken drapery, mattresses richly embroidered,
    Spacious enough for two, free in a wide room it stands.
Then let Jupiter get more joy from his Juno, a mortal
    Anywhere in this world know more contentment than I.
We enjoy the delights of the genuine naked god, Amor,
    And our rock-a-bye bed's rhythmic, melodious creak.

II

Honour whomever you please! But I at last am in safety!
    Beautiful ladies, and you, men of the elegant world,
Ask about uncles and aunts and second cousins and great-aunts,
    Then, after talk that's prescribed, start the wearisome game.
And the rest of you too, farewell, in large and in little
    Circles, who more than once brought me close to despair.
Pointless, political, gabble each commonplace current opinion
    Which across Europe incensed hounds the lone wanderer's track.
So once the ditty *Malbrouk* pursued the travelling Briton,
    First from Paris to Leghorn, then from Livorno to Rome,
Thence to Naples; and though he were now to sail off to far Smyrna,
    'Malbrouk' would welcome him there! 'Malbrouk' ring out on the quay.
And no differently I wherever I went had to hear the
    People scold and complain, curse the corruption of kings.
Now in vain you will try to find me, secure in the refuge
    Which to Amor, the prince, royal protection, I owe.
Here with his wings he conceals, covers his guest; the belovèd,
    Roman in thought, does not fear Gauls in their thundering rage.
Never yet she's enquired for news and rumours, but rather,
    Watchful, attends to the man, learns all his wishes and needs.
She delights in her friend, the vigorous, liberal stranger
    Who can tell her of snow, mountains, and timber-built house;
Shares the flames and the glow which she has awakened within him,
    Pleased that he does not stint gold as a Roman would do.
Richer now is her table; dresses and gowns are not lacking,
    Nor a carriage that waits close to the opera's door.
Mother and daughter alike are glad of the Northerner's presence.
    Roman bosom and limbs yield to barbarian rule.

III

Never, love, feel remorse that so quickly you gave yourself to me!
     Base, rest assured, I should be, brash, to esteem you the less.
Amor's arrows are various, variously strike: they may scratch you,
     And with a poison that creeps hearts will be aching for years.
Yet with strong flight-feathers, with heads that lately were sharpened
     Others pierce to the bone, kindling both marrow and blood.
In the heroic age, when gods and goddesses coupled,
     Lust was roused by one look, slaked as soon as conceived.
She, the goddess of love, do you think that long she considered
     When in Ida's grove she to Anchises was drawn?
Or had Luna been slow in kissing the beautiful sleeper,
     Jealous Aurora instead soon would have kissed him awake.
Hero caught sight of Leander when feasting was loud, and, impulsive,
     Hotly the lover plunged in, braved the black swell and the tide.
Rhea Silvia, the royal virgin, goes down to fetch water
     Out of Tiber, to be seized by the amorous god.
That's how Mars made sons for himself! – And the twins then are suckled
     By a she-wolf, and Rome calls herself Queen of the World.

IV

Pious we lovers are, and in silence revere all the spirits,
    Long to propitiate each, god and goddess alike.
And resemble in that you victors of Rome! To the gods of
    All the world's peoples you gave dwellings, a home far from home,
Whether black and severe out of ancient basalt Egyptians
    Or a Greek all in white shaped it, of marble, to charm.
Yet no timeless one bears any grudge if by discrimination
    One amongst them receives incense more precious from us.
Freely, indeed, we confess that still, as in past times, our prayers,
    Daily service to one, one above all, we devote.
Roguish, lively and serious we celebrate rituals in secret,
    Knowing that silence behoves all who are pledged to that cult.
Sooner by horrible acts to our heels we should summon and fasten
    Vengeful Furies, or else dare the harsh judgement of Zeus,
Suffer his rolling wheel or in fetters be clamped to the rock-face
    Than from that service of love sever our hearts and our minds.
And the goddess we serve? She is called Opportunity. Know her!
    Often to you she appears, always in different shapes.
Daughter of Proteus she'd like to think herself, mothered by Thetis,
    Hers by whose mutable guile many a hero was tricked.
So now her daughter tricks those inexperienced or timid,
    Teasing some in their sleep, flying past others who wake;
Gladly surrendering only to one who is quick, energetic.
    Gentle she is to that man, playful and tender and sweet.
Once she appeared to me too, as an olive-complexioned girl, whose
    Dark and plentiful hair, glistening, covered her brow,
Shorter ringlets curled round a neck that was graceful and slender,
    Wavy, unbraided hair rose from the top of her head.
And I recognized her; as she hurried I held her: and sweetly
    She, most willing to learn, soon paid me back each caress.
Oh, how delighted I was! – But enough, for that era is over.
    Now by you, Roman braids, tightly, all round, I'm entwined.

V

Happy now I can feel the classical climate inspire me,
    Past and present at last clearly, more vividly speak –
Here I take their advice, perusing the works of the ancients
    With industrious care, pleasure that grows every day –
But throughout the nights by Amor I'm differently busied,
    If only half improved, doubly delighted instead –
Also, am I not learning when at the shape of her bosom,
    Graceful lines, I can glance, guide a light hand down her hips?
Only thus I appreciate marble; reflecting, comparing,
    See with an eye that can feel, feel with a hand that can see.
True, the loved one besides may claim a few hours of the daytime,
    But in night hours as well makes full amends for the loss.
For not always we're kissing; often hold sensible converse.
    When she succumbs to sleep, pondering, long I lie still.
Often too in her arms I've lain composing a poem,
    Gently with fingering hand count the hexameter's beat
Out on her back; she breathes, so lovely and calm in her sleeping
    That the glow from her lips deeply transfuses my heart.
Amor meanwhile refuels the lamp and remembers the times when
    Likewise he'd served and obliged them, his triumvirs of verse.

VI

'How can you talk in that tone to me, so cruelly, crassly?
    Where you come from are all lovers as bitter and harsh?
If my name is mud, I must bear it; for am I not fallen,
    Guilty, in their eyes? But oh, fallen to no one save you!
These fine gowns are the evidence needed by envious neighbours
    That this widow has ceased mourning her husband indoors.
Rashly, didn't you come to this house many times in full moonlight,
    Grey, in your surplice-like cloak, hair in a clerical bun?
Didn't you, for a lark, make a point of selecting that costume?
    If a prelate it is, why, then that prelate is you.
In our spiritual Rome, believe it or not, but I'll swear it,
    Never a priest has received favours or solace from me.
Yes, I was poor, to my shame, and young, and well known to seducers.
    Falconieri, no less, gave me the eye more than once.
And a pimp of Albani's to Ostia now tried to lure me,
    Quattro Fontane now, always with notes that had weight.
Did this girl oblige? No, thanks. If there's one thing she's never
    Fancied, it's those who wear gaiters, the purple or red.
For, my father said, "In the end it's you girls who are diddled",
    Though my mother, I think, took a less serious view.
And, in the end, I have been. Diddled by you, when you're only
    Angry with me for show, scheming to jilt me and run.
Do. You men are unworthy of women. We carry the children
    Under our hearts, and there faithfulness also, for two.
But you men, as embracing you spill all your strength and your fervour
    At the same time you lose lovingness, too, in the act!'
So the loved one spoke, and swept up from his chair her one infant
    Son, whom she kissed and hugged, gazed at with tear-misted eyes.
Sitting there, how it shamed me to think that malevolent gossip
    By no fault but my own sullied an image so dear!
Darkly for moments only the fire will be smouldering, smoking,
    Drenched by water that damped, suddenly smothered its glow.
Very soon it revives, dispelling the murk of those vapours,
    And with mightier flames, all the more brightly, flares up.

VII

Oh, how happy I feel in Rome, when I think of the dreary
    Greyish enveloping days back in the North I've escaped,
Dull and heavy the sky on my head, like a smothering blanket,
    Colourless, shapeless the world, weary the eyes it repelled,
So that over my own self, to chart the dull mind's always gloomy,
    Profitless paths, I would brood, trapped in a circular maze.
Now the brighter azure, all radiant, illumines my forehead;
    Phoebus, the god, commands colours and shapes to stand out.
Starbright the night even gleams, and resounds with voluptuous singing
    And the moon to me shines brighter than northerly days.
Oh, what bliss for me, a mere mortal! A dream? Or the welcome,
    Father Jove, that you grant, your ambrosian house?
Here I lie, extending my hands as a suppliant to you,
    That I may touch your knees. Hear me, guest-sheltering Jove!
How I entered, I cannot say: it was Hebe that gathered
    Up the wandering man, drew me inside the great halls.
Was it your order to her – that she show in another hero?
    Did the lovely one err? Pardon her! Leave me the gain!
And your daughter Fortuna, she too! The most glorious presents
    She, as a girl, bestows, freely, as fancy commands.
Are you the welcoming god? If you are, from the heights of Olympus
    Do not expel your guest, back to the flatlands of earth!
'Poet, that's going too far! Come off it!' Well, yes, but this lofty
    Hill, the Capitoline is second Olympus to you.
Here put up with me, Jove, and let Hermes escort me down later,
    Past the Cestian tomb, softly to Orcus below.

VIII

When, belovèd, you tell me that as a child you were never
    Liked by people, and scorned by your own mother herself
All those years of your quiet growth, till mature, I believe you,
    In my mind's eye enjoy seeing the singular child.
Well, the vine-blossom too is deficient in shape and in colour,
    Yet to gods and mankind, mellow, the grape yields delight.

IX

Brightness autumnally shines from our rustic and sociable fireplace,
    Crackles and blazes – how swift – out of the faggots piled high.
More than ever tonight it is pleasing to me; for before to
    Charcoal the bundle's reduced, bending beneath so much ash,
She, my sweet girl, arrives. And both faggots and logs re-ignite now,
    So that their warmth makes our night festive and brilliantly lit.
Busily, early next morning she leaves the bed of our loving
    And from embers anew skilfully kindles more flames:
For to her more than others, my charmer, love's god gave the gift of
    Rousing up joy that just now, ember-like, spent, had collapsed.

X

Alexander and Caesar and Henry and Frederick, the great ones,
    Gladly would give in exchange half of the glory they won
If to each for one night, only one, I could offer such bedding;
    But by strict Hades' power – pity them! – those are held fast.
So rejoice, that you live, in the place that's been warmed by long loving,
    Now, before horribly Styx moistens your fugitive foot.

XI

Graces, on your pure altar it is that a poet is laying
    Down a few leaves to give thanks, offering buds of the rose.
And untroubled, assured. In his workshop an artist takes pleasure
    If to a pantheon too it always seems to expand.
His divine brow Jupiter lowers, and Juno's is lifted;
    Phoebus strides to the fore, shaking the curls on his head;
Drily Minerva looks down, and the not too scrupulous Hermes
    Casts a sidelong glance, roguish and tender at once.
Cytherea to Bacchus, the languidly dreamy, is raising
    Sweetly lascivious eyes, even in marble still moist;
Likes to recall his embrace, and seems by her look to be asking:
    Should not our glorious son also be here, at our side?

XII

Listen, darling: that shouting you hear in the Via Flaminia,
    Reapers it is, on their way back to the country and homes
Far from here, having finished the harvest for them, for the Romans
    Who disdain to wind garlands for Ceres themselves.
Festivals now no more are devoted to her, the great goddess,
    Giver of golden corn, rather than acorns, for fare,
Let the two of us honour that feast-day, rejoicing in private,
    Lovers, at least to themselves, being a nation conjoined.
Have you heard, perhaps, of that mystical celebration
    Which from Eleusis once followed a victor to Rome?
Hellenes founded the rite; and henceforth it has always been Hellenes,
    Even in Rome, who called out: 'Come into sanctified night!'
Those profane crept away, the expectant novice, though, trembled,
    Wrapped in a garment whose white signified pureness unstained.
Weirdly then the initiate wandered around, within circles
    Formed of strange shapes, in a dream seemed to be moving; for here
Serpents wriggled about, a procession of serious virgins
    Carried caskets all locked, garnished with ears of ripe corn.
Meaningfully the priests went about their performances, humming,
    While, impatient and awed, novices waited for light.
Not before many trials and tests were they finally granted
    Clues to the hallowed round's secret and curious signs.
What did the mystery mean, then? No more than this, that Demeter,
    Great though she was, did once yield to a hero's desires,
When to Iasion long since, a vigorous king of the Cretans,
    All her body's occult, inmost delights she vouchsafed.
Overjoyed was all Crete then. The marriage bed of the goddess
    Swelled with new growth, and the corn lushly weighed down all the fields.
Yet the rest of the world suffered famine; because in her transports
    Ceres completely forgot cares her high calling imposed.
Full of amazement each novice heard the incredible story,
    Made a sign to his love. – Now do you grasp it, my love?
It's a hallowed small place which that bushy-leaved myrtle tree shadows!
    Our contentedness harms no one, endangers no world.

XIII

Amor remains a rogue; and whoever trusts him will rue it!
　　　Canting he came to me: 'Trust me, just one more time.
You have earned my good will, by devoting your life and your writing
　　　Wholly to me and my praise. Gratitude now is your due.
Look, I have followed you even to Rome; and my wish is to render
　　　Adequate service to you, here, in a foreign domain.
Every tourist complains of the hospitality offered;
　　　Recommended by me, sweetly he's entertained.
At the rubble of ancient buildings you gape in amazement,
　　　And with a purpose explore Rome's every sanctified nook.
Even more you revere the worthy relics of artists,
　　　Those, I mean, whom at work always I used to look up.
Their creations – I shaped them myself! Excuse me, but this time
　　　I'm not boasting. You'll grant that what I'm saying is true.
Now that more laxly you serve me, where is the beauty of outline,
　　　Richness of colour, depth, glow your inventions possessed?
Are you thinking of doing more work now, my friend? Well, the school of
　　　Greece remains open, the years never have bolted its gates.
I, its teacher, am agelessly young, and I favour the youthful.
　　　Not prematurely wise, lively I'd like you to be.
Understand me. The ancient was new when those happy ones flourished!
　　　Only live happily, so making the past live in you.
Matter for song do you look for? Well, I alone can provide it
　　　And the afflatus, high style, only from love can be learnt.'
So the sophist argued. And who could refute him? And, sadly,
　　　I was brought up to obey when my superior commands. –
Treacherous, now he's true to his promise, grants matter for poems,
　　　Oh, and robs me of time, energy, reason at once.
Looks and pressure of hands, and kisses and comforting small-talk,
　　　Syllables fraught with sweet sense always we lovers exchange.
Lispings turn into converse here, into eloquence, lovely, our stammers;
　　　Void of both metre and rhyme, that sort of hymn dies away.
You, Aurora, how well once I knew you, as friend of the Muses!
　　　Dawn, even you has the knave Amor seduced, then, you too?

As his friend you appear to me now, at his bidding you wake me,
    There, at his altar, to greet, praise the resplendence of day.
Her abundance of curls on my breast I find there; her head lies
    Pressed, at rest on the arm made for encircling her neck.
What a joyful awakening, did but the hours of reflection
    Wholly preserve and recall pleasures that rocked us to sleep! –
In her drowsing she stirs now and slips to the bed's wider spaces,
    Turned away; nonetheless leaving her hand in my hand.
Always the love that unites us is heartfelt, and constant our craving,
    If alternation there is, lust's it is only, not ours.
One little squeeze of her hand, and the eyes I adore will reopen,
    Letting me gaze again. – No! Rather her shape I'll peruse!
Eyes, remain closed! You confuse me, intoxicate, rob me too soon of
    Joys that for quiet minds pure contemplation reserves.
How sublime these proportions! How nobly moulded her limbs are!
    If Ariadne slept so, Theseus, how could you run off?
Only one kiss on these lips! And, Theseus, just try now to leave her!
    Look in her eyes! She's awake! Never again you'll escape.

XIV

Light the lamp for me, boy! – 'But there's daylight; you'll only be wasting
    Oil and wick. So why close shutters at this time of day?
Not behind the mountain, but only these houses, the sun has
    Gone. Before angelus rings there's a good half-hour still left.'
Wretch! Now get moving, obey! My girl it is I'm awaiting.
    Comfort me meanwhile, small lamp, amiable herald of night!

XIVa

Two most dangerous serpents, *bêtes noires* of a chorus of poets,
    For millennia were known, fêted aghast by these names:
Python, you, and you, the Lernaean Hydra! But thanks to
    Capable gods and their strong hands you were beaten and killed.
With your fiery breath and your froth you no longer ravage
    Flocks and meadows and woods, fields newly golden with corn.
Yet what malevolent god in his wrath has more lately afflicted
    Us with the monstrous birth bred out of venomous mire?
Everywhere it intrudes; in the prettiest, neatest of gardens
    Slily the horror lurks, seizes all those who seek joy.
You, Hesperian dragon, I hail, for at least you showed courage,
    Boldly defending from theft apples, those golden ones, there!
Nothing this one defends, though; and where it's encountered, confronted,
    Garden and fruit will have proved not worth defending at all.
Hidden in shrubs, it proceeds by stealth and pollutes the well-springs,
    Frothing, to poison turns Amor's quivering dew.
Count yourself lucky, Lucretius, able to do without passion,
    To renounce it, and yet trust any body you chose!
And you, Propertius, were blessed. Your slave went out to fetch harlots
    Down from the Aventine Hill, out of the Tarpeian Grove,
And if Cynthia surprised you in one of those flagrant embraces
    Unfaithful she found you, true; yet found you healthy at least.

These days, a man will think twice before breaking a faith that's grown boring.
    Those whom love does not bind caution as surely deters.
And on home ground, who knows? Any pleasure at all has grown risky.
    Nowhere in women's laps heads can be laid without fear.
Marital beds are not safe now, adulterous beds are not safe now,
    Husband, lover and wife, each is a danger to each.
Oh, that golden age! When Jupiter still from Olympus
    Now to Semele went, now with Callisto could meet,
His concern it was also to find that the sanctified temple's
    Threshold was clean when he, loving and potent, came in.
Oh, how would Juno have raged if in love-combat her husband
    Foully against her had used weapons with poisonous tips.
Still not utterly, though, have old pagans like us been forsaken,
    Even now there's one god hovering over our earth,
Busy, quick off the mark, so you know him, we all do, and honour
    Him, the herald of Zeus, Mercury, healer of men.
Though the father's temples collapsed, their symmetrical columns
    Scarcely now mark the site glorious once and revered,
Yet the son's will stand, and for ages yet without number
    There will the suppliants come, jostling the ones who give thanks.
One thing only in secret I crave, to the Graces addressing
    This one prayer that wells, fervent and deep, from the heart:
Always protect my own little garden, ward off, I implore you,
    Every evil from me; touched by the hand of the rogue,
Amor, at all times grant me, whenever I trust myself to him,
    Pleasure unmixed with cares, bliss without peril or fear.

XV

Caesar, I think, would never have dragged me to far-away Britons,
    Easily Florus instead into the taverns of Rome!
It's those dismal fogs of the North. Still I find them more loathsome
    Than a whole work-team of keen Mediterranean fleas.
And from today more devoutly than ever I'll celebrate wineshops,
    Osterie, as inns aptly by Romans are called;
For today one showed me my darling, her uncle beside her,
    He whom so often the dear hoodwinks to dally with me.
Here was our table, the usual circle of Germans around it,
    Next to her mother my love, seating herself over there,
Shifted the bench many times and cleverly managed to turn it
    So that one half of her face, all of her neck was in view.
Raising her voice rather more than do ladies in Rome, she took up the
    Bottle, looking at me, poured, when the glass was not there,
Spilling wine on the table, and then with her delicate fingers
    Over the table-top drew circles in liquid, and loops.
With her own she entwined my name; and attentively always
    Those small fingers I watched, she well aware that I did.
Lastly a Roman five she signalled resourcefully, nimbly,
    With an upright in front. Quickly, the signal received,
Circle through circle she wound to erase the letters and symbols,
    Yet that precious FOUR lingered, impressed on my eyes.
Silent I sat there meanwhile, biting my lips that were sore now,
    Partly from mischievous joy, partly from burning desire.
First, the few hours until nightfall; then four long hours of more waiting!
    Sun up above, still you keep watch on your city of Rome!
Nothing greater you've seen and never will see a thing greater,
    Just as Horace your priest promised at one time, inspired.
But today, for once, do not stay, but avert your glances
    Soon from the Seven Hills, willing, for once, to depart!
For the sake of one poet curtail the magnificent daylight
    Which with eyes all aflame painters so relish and crave;
Glowing, take one more brief look at the palaces' lofty proportions,
    Cupolas, pillars and, last, up at the obelisks' tops;

Eagerly seek the sea and plunge in, all the sooner tomorrow
 Once again to behold age-old and godlike delight;
All these shores so moist, and so long overgrown with tall rushes,
 All these heights for so long shaded with bushes and trees.
Few small hovels at first they revealed; then all of a sudden
 Peopled you saw them, with crowds, fortunate brigands, they teemed.
Every manner of thing then they hauled to these parts and assembled;
 Hardly the rest of the globe now you found worthy of note.
Saw a world rise up here and then saw a world here in ruins,
 Out of the ruins once more almost a greater world rise!
So that a long time yet by you I may see it illumined,
 Let the Fate be slow, spinning that life-thread of mine.
All the quicker, however, the hour so invitingly signalled! –
 Rapt, do I hear it now? No, but the third hour has struck.
So, dear Muses, once more you've beguiled the length of my waiting,
 Tedious time-span that kept lover and lover apart.
Now farewell! As I hurry away, not afraid to offend you:
 Proud you are, but to him, Amor, will always defer.

XVI

'Dear one, this morning, why weren't you there as agreed, at the vineyard?
 On my own, as I said, there I was waiting for you.' –
Love, I was going in; when whom should I see but your uncle
 Prying between the vines, this way and that, as he turned.
Quickly I crept away. 'But how foolish of you! What an error!
 To mistake a scarecrow for him! Run for it, too! When the thing
Was a patchwork we made out of canes and old rags, in a hurry,
 Hard I worked at it too, only to spite my own face.'
Well, the old man had his way, and scared off a most feckless
 Bird, for the moment, that steals both from his garden and niece.

XVII

Many noises annoy me, but most of them all still I loathe the
    Barking of dogs; on my ear, yapping and whining, it grates.
Yet there's one dog that now I can hear with blithe satisfaction
    Yapping and barking, the dog trained by my neighbour to watch.
For it barked at my girl when one night she was softly, so softly
    Stealing into my room; almost it gave us away.
Now, whenever I hear it at once I think: she is coming!
    Or I think of the time when the awaited one came.

XVIII

One thing I find more annoying than anything else, but another
    Is abhorrent to me, so that each fibre revolts
At the thought of it merely. What are they? My friends, I'll confess it:
    Most annoying to me, nights spent alone in my bed.
Wholly abhorrent when walking love's pathways in secret the fear that
    Under the roses of bliss snakes and their venom may hide,
When at the very moment of pleasure's consummate surrender
    Apprehension comes lisping to heads as they sink.
That is why in Faustina my happiness lies; she most gladly
    Shares my bed, and requites strictly my faith with her own.
Challenging hurdles may suit the hot rashness of youth; what I like is
    Long to enjoy in assured comfort what once I possess.
What a blessing it is! We exchange reliable kisses,
    Safely take in and give out fusions of breath and of life.
So the long nights through we delight; so we lie and listen –
    Gale, heavy rain or shower – heart pressed up against heart;
So till dawn slowly breaks; and the hours to us bring renewal,
    Blossom we have not seen, festively garland our day.
Quirites, do not begrudge me such happiness; rather on all may
    This, the first and the last blessing be heaped by the god.

XIX

Hard it is to maintain our good name; for with Amor, my master,
  Only too well I'm aware, Fama is always at odds.
And I also know how it started, their mutual hatred.
  Very old stories they are, which I will tell all the same.
Always a powerful goddess, but socially always *non grata*,
  Fama was shunned because always she wants her own way;
So it came about that at every divine convocation
  Brazen-voiced she put off everyone else who was there.
Overreaching herself, for instance, at one time she boasted
  She had wholly enslaved Jove's most illustrious son.
'All in good time, O father of gods', she cried out, all exultant,
  'Back to you I shall bring Hercules, only reborn.
Not the Hercules, mind you, whom you with Alcmene engendered;
  His devotion to me makes him a god now on earth.
When to Olympus he looks you may think it's your knees, the majestic
  That he seeks; but it's me only, forgive me, that there
Up in aether he seeks; and, most worthy of men, to be worthy
  Only of me does his foot skim those untrodden terrains; –
But in turn on his travels I meet him half-way, and his praises
  I proclaim in advance, never awaiting the deed.
Me one day you shall marry to him; let the Amazon's victor
  Also be mine, and with joy him I shall hail as my spouse.'
Silence all round; no one was keen to provoke her, the braggart,
  Who, enraged, will think up, promptly, some wounding retort.
Amor escaped her notice: slunk off, and with minimal effort
  Soon had the hero engaged, and with a beauty, elsewhere.
Now he disguises his couple; on her shoulders loads the whole lion's
  Burdensome pelt, and leans next to it, somehow, the club.
Then with flowers he studs the resistant hair of the hero,
  Gives him a distaff to grip. Hercules bears with the joke.
So very soon he completes the derisive tableau; and careering
  Right through Olympus, shouts: 'Wonderful deeds have been done!
Never has earth or heaven, and never the sun that's untiring,
  Seen on its infinite course miracles equal to these.'

Everyone hurried, believing the mischievous boy, for in earnest
 He had seemed to speak; even she, Fama, must rush to the scene.
Guess who was tickled to know of the hero's discomfiting blunder!
 Juno it was. And she beamed favour at Amor for once.
Fama, beside her, stood there how shamed, how embarrassed, despairing,
 Though at first she laughed: 'Gods, these are nothing but masks!
I know better. It can't be my hero. We've all been made fools of
 By mere actors!' But soon sadly she saw that it was.
Not one thousandth so great was Vulcan's anger at seeing
 His little wife all enmeshed, caught with her militant friend,
When, exquisitely timed, the sagacious netting was tightened,
 Quickly constricting the clasped, holding them fast in their lust.
How delighted were Bacchus and Mercury; freely admitting,
 Youthful both, that to lie snug on that fine woman's breast
Was an idea not repulsive to them. And they begged the god Vulcan:
 'No, don't release them yet! Let's have another good look!'
And the old blacksmith, cuckolded anyway, held them more tightly. –
 As for Fama, she fled, promptly, and thoroughly vexed.
Since that time the feud I have mentioned has raged unabated:
 Hardly she's picked her man, after him chases the boy.
Him who most worships her, most efficiently, surely he catches;
 And he will compromise worst those whose righteousness shines.
Those who try to escape he leads on from bad things to worse things:
 Girls he'll offer to them; but, if misled, they decline,
From his bow they'll endure a shower of indignant arrows;
 Man he'll inflame for man, drive a man's lust towards beasts.
One who's ashamed of the god first must suffer; and hypocrites find that
 Bitter relish he's mixed into their crimes and distress.
But she too, the goddess, with keen eyes and keen ears pursues him.
 Only to see him with you wins you her lifelong ill will,
With her grave or contemptuous face she'll abash you, with iron
 Rigour condemn the house Amor presumes to frequent.
So it is with me too: I'm beginning to feel it; the goddess,
 Jealous, begins to pry into my secret affairs.
Yet the ancient law still holds good: I revere in silence –
 For the Greeks, as I must, paid for the quarrels of kings.

XX

Men distinguished by strength, by a frank and courageous nature,
 All the more, it would seem, need to be deeply discreet!
Secrecy, you that subdue a whole city! And rule over peoples,
 Tutelar goddess to me, leading me safely through life,
How my fate is reversed now! When, all facetious, the Muses,
 Jointly with Amor, the rogue, loosen the lips that were sealed.
Hard enough it's already to cover up royal disgraces!
 Crown or Phrygian cap, neither now serves to conceal
Midas's long pointed ears. Any servant of his will have noticed,
 And at once feels oppressed, awed by the secret within.
Deep he'd like to bury it, and be rid of the worrying knowledge,
 Yet mere earth will not keep secrets like that one intact,
Rushes shoot from the ground and they whisper and sough in the breezes:
 'Midas, Midas the king, Midas has long pointed ears!'
Now it is harder for me to preserve my more beautiful secret,
 Given such fullness of heart, easily lips overflow.
To no woman friend I can tell it; for she would reproach me;
 In no male friend confide: danger could come from that source.
To proclaim my rapture to groves and the echoing hillsides
 I'm not young enough now, lonely enough, come to that.
So to you, my couplets, my elegies, let me entrust it,
 How she delights me by day, fills me with rapture by night.
She, sought after by many men, skilfully shuns all the snares which
 Brashly the bold ones lay, subtly the shame-faced and sly;
Lithe and clever, she gives them the slip, for she knows all the footpaths
 Where her lover will wait, listening, confident, keen.
Luna, be late, for she comes! And make sure that our neighbour won't see her;
 Rustle, leaves, in the shrubs! No one must hear her light step.
And, dear elegies, you, may you flourish and blossom, be cradled
 Warm in the lightest of breaths lovingly wafted by air,
Then give away to all Rome, as they did, those garrulous rushes,
 Secrets one fortunate pair treasured and kept to themselves.

from

VENETIAN EPIGRAMS

15

Fantasts make converts enough and stir a whole crowd into frenzy,
    While the rational man counts on the love of a few.
Miracle-working pictures are usually bungled as painting;
    Works of the mind and of art do not exist for the mob.

17

True, among Germany's princes my own is accounted a small one,
    Short and narrow his realm, moderate only his power.
But if the others applied theirs at home and abroad as my prince does,
    Ah, to be German among Germans, what endless delight!
Why did you laud him, in that case, when actions and works are his glory,
    And your reverence, too, many could whisper, is bribed?
For to me he has given what great ones most rarely have granted,
    Favour, leisure and trust, fields and a garden and house.
Gratitude only to him I have owed, and my needs were most urgent,
    Since, as a poet, I lacked skill from which profit accrues.
All of Europe may praise me, but what have I gained from all Europe?
    Nothing! No, I have paid, dearly enough, for my verse.
Germany aped what I wrote, and in France they were eager to read me,
    England, you kindly received this hypochondriac guest.
But what good does it do me if even a Chinaman's fingers,
    Sensitive, hesitant, paint Werther and Charlotte on glass?
Never an emperor asked for, and never a king cared a jot for
    Me. My Maecenas was he, and my Augustus, combined.

18

One man's life, what is it? Yet thousands of talkers will batten,
    Speculate on the man, what he achieved, by what means.
As for a poem, it's less; yet a thousand will praise and enjoy it,
    Thousands find fault. My friend, just keep on living, and write!

20

Your apostles of Liberty, always their sort has repelled me,
    Absolute power for himself each of them sought in the end.
If you wish to free many, then dare to do service to many.
    'Dare? So it's dangerous work?' Questioner, try it and see!

31

Why do they teem so, these people, and yell? It's to feed that they bustle,
    Procreate children and then feed them as well as they can.
Tourist, take note of that and, back in your homeland, do likewise!
    Try and pretend as he may, no man achieves more than that.

33

Eros, well I know you, if anyone does! With your torch you
    Come to us, and it shines brightly for us in the dark.
Soon, however, you lead us down intricate paths; when we need it
    Most of all, your bright torch, not to be trusted, goes out.

53

France's pitiable fate, the great may reflect on its meaning.
    Yet the little still more ought to consider that plight.
True, many great ones perished; but who protected the masses
    From the masses? Then mob proved the oppressor of mob.

55   ·

'Tell us, aren't we right? We've no choice but to hoodwink the rabble.
    Only look how uncouth, look how ferocious its ways!'
Crudely hoodwink a man, and uncouth, ferocious you'll make him.
    No, be honest with them. Human they'll grow by degrees.

77

So you dabble in botany, optics? How can you, a poet?
    Don't you feel better employed touching a sensitive heart?
Oh, those sensitive hearts. Any charlatan knows how to touch them.
    No, let my one joy be this, Nature, to touch upon you!

LATER POEMS

The Metamorphosis of Plants

Overwhelming, belovèd, you find all this mixture of thousands,
    Riot of flowers let loose over the garden's expanse;
Many names you take in, and always the last to be spoken
    Drives out the one heard before, barbarous both to your ear.
All the shapes are akin and none is quite like the other;
    So to a secret law surely that chorus must point,
To a sacred enigma. Dear friend, how I wish I were able
    All at once to pass on, happy, the word that unlocks!
Growing consider the plant and see how by gradual phases,
    Slowly evolved, it forms, rises to blossom and fruit.
From the seed it develops as soon as the quietly fertile
    Womb of earth sends it out, sweetly released into life,
And to the prompting of light, the holy, for ever in motion,
    Like the burgeoning leaves' tenderest build, hands it on.
Single, dormant the power in the seed was; the germ of an image,
    Closed in itself, lay concealed, prototype curled in the husk,
Leaf and root and bud, although colourless yet, half-amorphous;
    Drily the nucleus so safeguards incipient life,
Then, aspiring, springs up, entrusting itself to mild moisture,
    Speedily raises itself out of encompassing night.
Single, simple, however, remains the first visible structure;
    So that what first appears, even in plants, is the child.
Following, rising at once, with one nodule piled on another,
    Always the second renews only the shape of the first.
Not the same, though, for ever; for manifold – you can observe it –
    Mutably fashioned each leaf after the last one unfolds,
More extended, spikier, split into lances or segments
    Which, intergrown before, lay in the organ below.
Only now it attains the complete intended perfection
    Which, in many a kind, moves you to wonder, admire.
Many-jagged and ribbed, on a lusciously, fully fleshed surface,
    Growth so lavishly fed seems without limit and free.

Forcefully here, however, will Nature step in to contain it,
    Curbing rankness here, gently perfecting the shapes.
Now more slowly the sap she conducts, and constricts the vessels,
    And at once the form yields, with diminished effects.
Calmly the outward thrust of the spreading leaf-rims recedes now,
    While, more firmly defined, swells the thin rib of the stalks.
Leafless, though, and swift the more delicate stem rises up now,
    And, a miracle wrought, catches the onlooker's eye.
In a circular cluster, all counted and yet without number
    Smaller leaves take their place, next to a similar leaf.
Pushed close up to the hub now, the harbouring calyx develops
    Which to the highest of forms rises in colourful crowns.
Thus in fulness of being does Nature now glory, resplendent,
    Limb to limb having joined, all her gradations displayed.
Time after time you wonder as soon as the stalk-crowning blossom
    Sways on its slender support, gamut of mutable leaves.
Yet the splendour becomes an announcement of further creation.
    Yes, to the hand that's divine colourful leaves will respond.
And it quickly furls, contracts; the most delicate structures
    Twofold venture forth, destined to meet and unite.
Wedded now they stand, those delighted couples, together.
    Round the high altar they form multiple, ordered arrays.
Hymen, hovering, nears, and pungent perfumes, exquisite,
    Fill with fragrance and life all the environing air.
One by one now, though numberless, germs are impelled into swelling
    Sweetly wrapped in the womb, likewise swelling, of fruit.
Nature here closes her ring of the energies never-exhausted
    Yet a new one at once links to the circle that's closed,
That the chain may extend into the ages for ever,
    And the whole be infused amply with life, like the part.
Look, belovèd, once more on the teeming of so many colours,
    Which no longer may now fill with confusion your mind.
Every plant now declares those eternal designs that have shaped it,
    Ever more clearly to you every flower-head can speak.
Yet if here you decipher the holy runes of the goddess,
    Everywhere you can read, even though scripts are diverse:

Let the grub drag along, the butterfly busily scurry,
    Imaging man by himself alter the pre-imposed shape.
Oh, and consider then how in us from the germ of acquaintance
    Stage by stage there grew, dear to us, habit's long grace,
Friendship from deep within us burst out of its wrapping,
    And how Amor at last blessed it with blossom and fruit.
Think how variously Nature, the quietly forming, unfolding,
    Lent to our feelings now this, now that so different mode!
Also rejoice in this day. Because love, our holiest blessing
    Looks for the consummate fruit, marriage of minds, in the end,
One perception of things, that together, concerted in seeing,
    Both to the higher world, truly conjoined, find their way.

Nature and Art

Nature, it seems, must always clash with Art
And yet, before we know it, both are one;
I too have learned: Their enmity is none,
Since each compels me, and in equal part.

Hard, honest work counts most! And once we start
To measure out the hours and never shun
Art's daily labour till our task is done
Freely again may Nature move the heart.

So too all growth and ripening of the mind:
To the pure heights of ultimate consummation
In vain the unbound spirit seeks to flee.

Who seeks great gain leaves easy gain behind.
None proves a master but by limitation
And only law can give us liberty.

Sicilian Song

Eyes bright and cherry-black,
If you but blink
The tallest houses crack,
Whole cities fall;
And do you think perhaps
This cob wall of my heart,
Mere straw and clay and gravel,
Will not collapse?

Found

Once in the forest
I strolled content,
To look for nothing
My sole intent.

I saw a flower,
Shaded and shy,
Shining like starlight,
Bright as an eye.

I went to pluck it;
Gently it said:
Must I be broken,
Wilt and be dead?

Then whole I dug it
Out of the loam
And to my garden
Carried it home,

There to replant it
Where no wind blows.
More bright than ever
It blooms and grows.

Apothegmata. Orphic

DAIMON, *Daemon*

As on the day that gave you to this world
The sun stood, in relation to the planets,
So from that moment forth and forth you throve
According to the law that ruled your birth.
So you must be, from selfhood there's no fleeing,
So Sibyls, prophets long ago declared;
And neither time nor any power can break it,
The living pattern latent in all growth.

TYCHE, *Chance*

Yet that strict limit by a mutable force,
Around and in us, smoothly is avoided;
Not single you remain, by others you are formed
And are disposed to do as others do.
In life this thing falls vacant, that turns round,
It's trivial stuff, and you will trifle through it.
The quiet circle of the years has closed,
The lamp awaits its kindling by the flame.

EROS, *Love*

And come it will! – He hurtles down from heaven
To which from ancient bleakness he arose,
He hovers close to you on airy plumage
Round breast and brow, streaks through a vernal day,
Now seems to flee, but will reverse his fleeing,
Makes you feel well in woe, so weirdly sweet.
Many's the heart by general heights undone,
The noblest, though, devotes itself to One.

ANANKE, *Compulsion*

And now it's back to what the planets willed:
Law and restriction; so that all we will
Is only willing what we had to will,
And by that will our wilfulness is stilled:
What it liked best the heart now scolds away,
Will and caprice to a hard Must give way.
So, would-be-free-willed, after many a year
We're still more tightly tethered than we were.

ELPIS, *Hope*

Yet such a limit's, such a brazen wall's
Most odious door in time will be unlocked,
So let it stand, for all its rocky face!
A being that is light, unbridled, stirs:
From covering cloud, from mist and drizzly showers
She lifts us up, on wings both hers and ours:
You know her well, she soars through every zone:
One wingbeat – and whole aeons we've outflown.

At Midnight

At midnight, far from gladly at that hour,
A small, small boy along the churchyard I
Walked to my father's vicarage; star on star,
Oh how they shone, too richly lit the sky;
    At midnight.

When later I, moved farther though not far,
Must see the loved one, must because she drew me,
Above me stars and northern lights at war,
Going and coming I felt bliss flow through me;
    At midnight.

Until at last the full moon made a rift
So bright, so clear within the dark of me,
And even thought, grown willing, limber, swift
Embraced both past and future easily;
    At midnight.

Epirrhema

Always in observing nature
Look at one and every creature;
Nothing's outside that's not within,
For nature has no heart or skin.
All at once that way you'll see
The sacred open mystery.

True seeming is the joy it gives,
The joy of serious playing;
No thing is single, if it lives,
But multiple its being.

Antepirrhema

Therefore with eyes not arrogant view
The eternal weaver's artistry,
How one tread moves a thousand threads,
This way and that the shuttles flit,
The many threads, converging, knit,
One lever links the myriads.
This not by patchwork she contrives
But from eternity derives,
So that the eternal Master may
Order the woof's consistency.

Parabasis

Many years ago the mind
Chose of glad prerogatives
Zealously to search and find
How, creating, Nature lives.
An eternal One and All
In her multiple shapes appear:
Small the great thing, great the small,
Each according to its kind;
Ever changing, ever constant,
Near and far and far and near,
Forming thus and thus transforming –
And to marvel I am here.

One and All

In boundlessness to lose and find
Themselves, the single are inclined,
Shedding the irksome bond, the tight.
Free of strong willing, wild desiring,
Imperious must and hard requiring,
In our unselfing we delight.

World soul, you come, flow into us!
Then with the world's own spirit thus
To grapple is our highest call.
Good spirits, master-minds indeed
Gently, by sympathy, will lead
To him who made and still makes all.

To recreate the once created,
Lest it grow rigid, crenellated,
Is live, eternal doing's end.
And what was not, now craves new birth
As a pure sun, a colourful earth –
Never to rest, never to pend.

No, active, it shall stir, create,
First shape itself and then mutate;
It only seems to pause, hang still.
The eternal works in all that's wrought:
For all to nothingness is brought
If changeless being is its will.

The Bridegroom

At midnight, I was sleeping, in my breast
My fond heart lay awake, as though it were day;
Day broke: as though by falling night oppressed
I thought: what's day to me, bring what it may?

Since she was lacking; all my toil and strife
For her alone patiently I'd withstood
Throughout the hot noon hours. What quickening life
In the cool evening! Blessed it was, and good.

from
WEST-EASTERN DIVAN

Hegira

North and West and South are breaking,
Thrones are bursting, kingdoms shaking:
Flee, then, to the essential East,
Where on patriarch's air you'll feast!
There to love and drink and sing,
Drawing youth from Khizr's spring.

Pure and righteous there I'll trace
To its source the human race,
Prime of nations, when to each
Heavenly truth in earthly speech
Still by God himself was given,
Human brains not racked and riven.

When they honoured ancestors,
To strange doctrine closed their doors;
Youthful bounds shall be my pride,
My thought narrow, my faith wide.
And I'll find the token word,
Dear because a spoken word.

Mix with goatherds in dry places,
Seek refreshment in oases
When with caravans I fare,
Coffee, shawls, and musk my ware;
Every road and path explore,
Desert, cities and seashore;

*

Dangerous track, through rock and scree:
Hafiz, there you'll comfort me
When the guide, enchanted, tells
On the mule's back, your ghazels,
Sings them for the stars to hear,
Robber bands to quail with fear.

Holy Hafiz, you in all
Baths and taverns I'll recall,
When the loved one lifts her veil,
Ambergris her locks exhale.
More: the poet's love song must
Melt the houris, move their lust.

Now, should you begrudge him this,
Even long to spoil such bliss,
Poets' words, I'd have you know,
Round the gate of Eden flow,
Gently knocking without rest,
Everlasting life their quest.

Blessèd Longing

Tell it only to the wise,
For the crowd at once will jeer:
That which is alive I praise,
That which longs for death by fire.

Cooled by passionate love at night,
Procreated, procreating,
You have known the alien feeling
In the calm of candlelight;

Gloom-embraced will lie no more,
By the flickering shades obscured,
But are seized by new desire,
To a higher union lured.

Then no distance holds you fast;
Winged, enchanted, on you fly,
Light your longing, and at last,
Moth, you meet the flame and die.

Never prompted to that quest:
Die and dare rebirth!
You remain a dreary guest
On our gloomy earth.

Unbounded

What makes you great is that you cannot end,
And never to begin you are predestined.
Your song revolves as does the starry dome,
Beginning, end for ever more the same;
And what the middle brings will prove to be
What last remains and was initially.

Of poets' joys you are the one true source,
Wave after numberless wave you give to verse.
Lips that of kissing never tire,
Song from the breast that sweetly wells,
A throat that's never quenched, on fire,
An honest heart that freely tells.

And though the whole world were to sink,
Hafiz, with you, with you alone
I will compete! Delight, despair,
Let us, the twins, entirely share!
Like you to love, like you to drink
My life and pride I here declare.

Self-fuelled now, my song, ring truer!
For you are older, you are newer.

Submerged

Full of crisp curls, a head so round! –
And if in such abundant hair I may
With full hands travel, or return to stay,
Down to my inmost being I feel sound.
If forehead, eyebrow, eye and lips I kiss,
Ever again renewed, I'm sore with bliss.
The five comb-fingers, where should their roaming end?
Already to those curls again they bend.
Nor do the ears refuse their part.
They are not flesh, they are not skin,
Such a love-gamut for tenderly bantering art!
No matter how fondled, here, within
One little head's abundant hair,
For ever forth and back you'll fare.
So, Hafiz, once you used to do,
And we embark on it anew.

Greeting

O what bliss came to me!
In the country I walked
Where Hudhud crosses the path.
The shells of the old sea,
Among stones I looked for their fossils;
Hudhud came running,
Raising his crest,
And stalked, teasingly,
Joking about the dead,
He, the living.
Hudhud, I said, really!
A fine bird you are.
Hurry then, hoopoe!
Hurry to tell
My belovèd that for ever
I'm hers.
When already
Between Solomon
And the Queen of Sheba
Long ago your part was the pimp's.

Gingo Biloba

This tree's leaf that from the East
To my garden's been entrusted
Holds a secret sense, and grist
To a man intent on knowledge.

Is it one, this thing alive,
By and in itself divided,
Or two beings who connive
That as one the world shall see them?

Fitly now I can reveal
What the pondered question taught me;
In my songs do you not feel
That at once I'm one and double?

On Laden Twigs

On laden twigs of bushes,
There, loved one, to be seen,
The fruit let this uncover,
Spiky, encased and green.

Long clenched they have been hanging
Self-unacquaintedly.
A bough that swaying wanders
Cradles them patiently.

Yet always from within them
The swelling seed has matured,
Longs to be out in the open,
Of sun and air assured.

The casing bursts, and joyful
Each one breaks loose from its trap;
So too my songs are dropping
Profusely into your lap.

Hatem to Zuleika

These, the finely penned,
Splendidly gilt-surrounded
You smiled at,
These presumptuous sheets;
Forgave my bragging
About your love and my
Achievement, made happy by you,
Forgave graceful self-praise.

Self-praise! Only to envy it stinks,
A sweet fragrance to friends
And one's own senses!

The pleasures of living are great,
Greater the pleasure in living.
When you, Zuleika,
Profusely delight me,
Throw me your passion
As though it were a ball
For me to catch
And throw back to you
My dedicated self:
That is a moment indeed!
And then I am torn from you
Now by the Frank, now the Armenian.

But for days on end,
For years now, I have been newly creating
A thousandfold your lavishments' fulness,
Untwisting the many-coloured string of my happiness,
Wound of a thousand threads
By you, Zuleika!

Here, in exchange,
Poetic pearls
That your passion's
Powerful swell
Cast up on life's
Deserted shore.
Delicately picked
With pointed fingers,
Interspersed with jewelled
Ornaments of gold,
Place them on your neck,
On your bosom!
The raindrops of Allah,
Grown ripe in modest shells.

Hatem to Zuleika

No longer on sheets of silk
Symmetrical rhymes I paint,
No longer frame them
In golden arabesques;
Imprinted on mobile dust
They are swept by the wind, but their power endures,
As far as the centre of Earth,
Riveted, bound to the soil.
And the wanderer will come,
The lover. If he enters
This place, all his limbs
Will feel the thrill.
'Here, before me, the lover loved.
Was it Medjun, the tender?
Farhad, the strong? Was it Djemil, the obstinate?
Or one of a thousand other
Happy, unhappy men?
He loved! I love as he loved.
I avenge him!'
But you, Zuleika, rest
On the delicate cushion
That I prepared for you and embellished.
And your limbs too, roused from their languor, thrill.
'It is he who calls me, Hatem,
And I call to you, O Hatem, Hatem!'

Echo

So proud it sounds when to the sun
Poets compare themselves, or to the Emperor;
Yet they conceal the drab, the dreary vision
When in dark nights they slink and cower.

Clotted and clogged by clouds in streaks,
At night it vanished, the heavens' most limpid blue;
Now pale and sunken are my cheeks
And my heart's tears are ashen-grey.

Don't leave me so to night, to loss,
My most-belovèd, my moonface, bright,
O you my candle, you my phosphorus,
You my sun's radiance, you my light!

Cold Comfort

At midnight I wept and sobbed
Because I lacked you.
Then night spirits came
And I was ashamed.
Night spirits, I said,
Weeping and sobbing
You find me whom you used
To pass by asleep.
Great possessions I've lost.
Don't think less well of me
Whom you used to call wise;
Great affliction besets him! –
And the night spirits
With long faces
Passed by,
Not caring a jot
Whether I'm wise or foolish.

Summer Night

POET

Look, the sun's gone down and vanished,
Yet the West is all a-glimmer,
How much longer still, I wonder,
Can it last, that golden shimmer?

CUP-BEARER

If you wish, sir, as your watchman
Here outside the tents I'll wait
To report to you the moment
When Night wins, the glow goes out.

For, I know, you love up-there-ness,
To peruse what is unending,
When those fires in dark-blue distance
One another are commending.

And the brightest claims no more than:
'In my place I shine, and rightly:
If more light the Lord had wished you,
You would shine like me, as brightly.'

For in God's eyes all is glorious,
Being great, beyond compare, He;
So all kinds of birds are sleeping
In the little nest or aerie.

Or, it could be, one is perching
Safe amid the cypress branches,
Lulled by warm and gentle breezes
Till the wafted dew-drop blanches.

Such has been your teaching, Master,
If not in those very phrases;
What from your lips I have gathered
Nothing from my heart erases.

Owl for your sake on this terrace
I will hoot it out, besotted,
Till the Northern constellation's
Twin-conjuncture I have spotted.

And by then it will be midnight,
When too often you're untiring;
And a splendour it will be then:
Both of us the All admiring.

POET

In this fragrance, true, and garden
Whole nights through will Bulbul chatter;
Yet a long time you could wait for
Night to clinch the larger matter.

At this season, that of Flora,
As the Roman people named her,
Our grass widow, pale Aurora,
Lust for Hesperus has inflamed her.

Look around! She comes. How swiftly
Over flowery fields has flitted!
Bright this side and bright the other,
Night's hard-pressed, by light outwitted.

And on soles how red and flimsy
After him in vain she's run –
Can't you hear an amorous snorting? –
Who's absconded with the sun.

Go inside, dear boy, and hurry,
Deep behind closed doors, no less,
For as Hesperus she wants you,
To seduce your loveliness.

'To my delight and wonderment'

To my delight and wonderment I
In the Koran saw a peacock feather lie:
Welcome, I thought, to that holy place
Formative Earth's rich masterpiece!
In you, as in the stars above
God's greatness in little things we can prove,
That He, who sees the world in space
His own eye's image could here impress
And so the flimsy down could grace
That kings themselves would scarcely try
To match the bird in majesty.
If in that glory humbly you rejoice,
You're worthy of the sanctum, of the choice.

'Let me weep'

Let me weep, hemmed in by night,
In the boundless desert.
Camels are resting, likewise the drivers,
Calculating in silence the Armenian is awake;
But I, beside him, calculate the miles
That separate me from Zuleika, reiterate
The annoying bends that prolong journeys.
Let me weep. It is no shame.
Weeping men are good.
Didn't Achilles weep for his Briseis?
Xerxes wept for his unfallen army;
Over his self-murdered darling
Alexander wept.
Let me weep. Tears give life to dust.
Already it's greening.

The Generous Man Is Cheated

The generous man is cheated,
The avaricious exploited,
The prudent led astray,
The sensible sucked dry,
The hard man outflanked,
The gullible hoodwinked.
Master it, that deceit:
Cheated, learn to cheat.

Admit: the Poets of the East

Admit: the poets of the East
Are greater than we of the West.
But the one thing in which we leave them behind
Is detestation of our own kind.

For Enduring Respect

For enduring respect what's wanted
Is bristles, well to the fore.
With hawks all sorts are hunted
But not the wild boar.

Never in Any Circumstance

Never in any circumstance
Let them induce you to refute.
Wise men fall into ignorance
When with the ignorant they dispute

MISCELLANEOUS EPIGRAMS

To Those Who Think Themselves Original

I

Somebody says: 'Of no school I am part,
Never to living master lost my heart;
Nor any more can I be said
To have learned anything from the dead.'
That statement – subject to appeal –
Means: 'I'm a self-made imbecile.'

II

My build from Father I inherit,
His neat and serious ways;
Combined with Mother's cheerful spirit,
Her love of telling stories.
Great-grandfather courted the loveliest,
His ghost won't leave me alone;
Great-grandmother liked fine jewels best,
This twitch I've also known.
If, then, no mortal chemist can
Divide the components from the whole,
What in the entirety of that man
Could you call original?

The Years

The years? A charming lot, I say.
Brought presents yesterday, bring presents today,
And so we younger ones maintain
The charming life that's led in Cockayne.
Then all of a sudden the years change their mind,
Are no longer obliging, no longer kind;
Won't give you presents, won't let you borrow,
Dun you today, and rob you tomorrow.

Society

From a social gathering, large and polite,
A quiet scholar came home one night.
Asked how he'd liked it, the scholar said:
'If they were books, I'd leave them unread.'

New Egg, Good Egg

Enthusiasm, my good sir,
Is like the oyster, I aver,
Which, if you do not eat it new,
Most probably will make you spew –
Unlike your herring, solid fare
That, pickled, keeps for many a year.

A But in It

How pleasant to guzzle all that's best,
If only one didn't have to digest.
Glorious to drink one's fill, and more,
If head and knees didn't make for the floor.
To shoot your opponent would be great fun
If only your opponent didn't have a gun;
And every girl would be ready to play
If that put someone else in the family way.

Old Age

Old Age? he is a gentleman,
Knocks on the door again and again,
But no one answers, calls: Come in!
And out in the cold his patience wears thin.
So he turns the doorknob, inside in a flash;
And now they tell you the fellow is brash.

'Whatever as a truth or fable'

Whatever as a truth or fable
To you a thousand books have shown
Is nothing but a Tower of Babel
Till love the binder makes it one.

'Were they not sun-akin'

Were they not sun-akin, our eyes,
To sunlight's glory they'd be blind;
Were they not in us, God's own energies,
How could divine things move our kind?

'In living as in knowing'

In living as in knowing, be
Intent upon the purest way;
When gale and current push you, pull you,
Yet they'll never overrule you;
Compass and pole-star, chronometer
And sun and moon you'll read the better,
With quiet joy, in your own fashion
Will reach the proper destination.
Especially if you don't despair
Because the course is circular:
A circumnavigator, hail
The harbour whence you first set sail.

'Did they appreciate'

'Did they appreciate the good in you?'
Well-feathered, away my arrow flew,
All of the sky wide-open to it.
Somewhere, something it must have hit.

'For him and her'

For him and her you find a name
And think you know them by the same.
Who sees more deeply will admit:
There's something anonymous in it.

'Would I were rid'

Would I were rid of all tradition
And wholly original;
But that's a rather large ambition
And leads to many a fall.
As one autochthonous I'd be
Most flattered to think it true,
If only myself most curiously
Were not tradition too.

True Enough: To the Physicist

'Into the core of Nature' –
O Philistine –
'No earthly mind can enter.'
The maxim is fine;
But have the grace
To spare the dissenter,
Me and my kind.
We think: in every place
We're at the centre.
'Happy the mortal creature
To whom she shows no more
Than the outer rind,'
For sixty years I've heard your sort announce.
It makes me swear, though quietly;
To myself a thousand times I say:
All things she grants, gladly and lavishly;
Nature has neither core
Nor outer rind,
Being all things at once.
It's yourself you should scrutinize to see
Whether you're centre or periphery.

Epitaphs

I

In boyhood I was tender and good,
In youth impulsive, with quick blood,
Promised to be a man.
I've loved and suffered. Readily,
With no regret, now down I lie
Because I can't go on.

II

In boyhood stubborn, withdrawn,
In youth presumptuous, suspicious,
When mature, an active man,
In old age reckless, capricious. –
On your gravestone they'll make out:
This one was human, never doubt!